Thank you to all who have followed along on this big stick adventure.
I hope this book inspires you to find adventure no matter
where you are in the world.

A huge thank you to my partner, Brandon, for keeping the kettle boiling and wood stove lit as I illustrated a majority of this book during a cold PNW winter and to my mother, Amy, and sister, Grayson, for editing the many versions!

Self-published by Gatlin Creatives in Bellingham, WA
ISBN 979-8-8692-2162-9
www.JoJotheAdventurePup.com
@JoJotheAdventurePup

JOJO THE ADVENTURE PUP spread his map on the ground,
excited to explore each state, where new adventures could be found.

He packed his bag with all types of gear
ready to take off and journey all year.

In ALASKA JoJo mushed many miles in the snow
on the Iditarod trail with huskies in tow.

Along the waters that separate a country and state,
he sailed with orcas into the straight.

In WASHINGTON JoJo spawned with salmon upriver,
underneath a volcano ready for winter.

To OREGON he dove off steep Haystack Rock,
alongside Pickle the Puffin and her flock.

In **CALIFORNIA** JoJo found a stick from the largest of trees,
and ran through the forest older than the seas.

After his flight to **HAWAII** he surfed Northshore's famous waves
alongside Tutu the turtle who has lived for decades!

In **ARIZONA** JoJo painted the most colorful desert
with his new friend Riley posed with a pheasant.

Below **NEVADA** he swam down deep in Lake Mead
to an airplane wreck covered in seaweed.

UTAH brought slot canyons carved by Escalante River
explored alongside a big horn sheep that never quivered.

To IDAHO he bathed in a hot spring with a moose,
underneath the shade of a giant spruce.

In MONTANA JoJo galloped with a Bison named Berry
on the Flathead Reservation's prairie.

WYOMING brought the most colorful spring,
surrounded by geysers, volcanoes, and other wild things.

In **COLORADO** JoJo camped on the tallest of peaks
and listened to the pikas scurry and squeak.

South to **NEW MEXICO** he floated with hundreds of balloons
just in time for the rise of the full moon.

In TEXAS JoJo howled up Paulo Duro Canyon with a coyote named Cucumber and his companions.

To OKLAHOMA he sat amongst the prairie dog holes, watching an Eastern Collared lizard go for a stroll.

On the KANSAS River JoJo rowed with Brewgan the dog
when out of no where splashed a slimy frog!

In NEBRASKA he rested in Toadstool Geologic Park,
gazing at the galaxies and stars deep in the dark.

In **SOUTH DAKOTA** JoJo dug through the Badland's colorful stones
and surprisingly uncovered a pile of bones.

Down **NORTH DAKOTA'S** steepest of trails he raced
Cashew the Cougar who took first place.

In MINNESOTA JoJo sailed under Lake Superior's northern lights,
taking in the magnificent sight.

Below IOWA he spelunked the Maquoketa Caves so tight,
before climbing towards the bright forest light.

In **MISSOURI** JoJo hiked along the Ozark Trail,
with his friend Broccoli the black bear.

To **ARKANSAS** he explored the stones made of sand,
carved by wind and water on the Bear Cave Trail's land.

In **LOUISIANA** JoJo zoomed along the largest swamp,
avoiding the alligators and their large chomps!

Along **MISSISSIPPI'S** Natchez Trace Parkway, he drove through the ridge,
racing a speedy barred owl over a bridge.

In ALABAMA JoJo traveled to Dauphin Island in the fall
to listen to over 400 species of birds make their call.

In FLORIDA JoJo went for a float in a spring so blue
atop a sea cow that didn't moo.

In **GEORGIA** JoJo prepared to hike the Appalachian Trail with Jack
who was carrying quite a large pack.

In **SOUTH CAROLINA** he kayaked along Congree National Park's waters
waving hello to the napping otters.

Along **NORTH CAROLINA** JoJo galloped with a wild horse named Tank,
on the dune filled shoreline of the Outer Banks.

Above **TENNESSEE** he flew through the fog and the vapor
finally seeing the Smoky Mountains thousands of acres.

In VIRGINIA JoJo climbed to the top of Birch Knob Tower
to see the mountains, valleys, and fields full of flower.

Deep in KENTUCKY JoJo crept in a cave armed with a light,
when a bat flew out and gave him quite a fright.

In ILLINOIS JoJo dove down Jackson Falls
while his friend Nelson climbed the rocky walls.

Heading north to WISCONSIN he strolled among the sunflowers
watching the colors change from the sun's golden hour

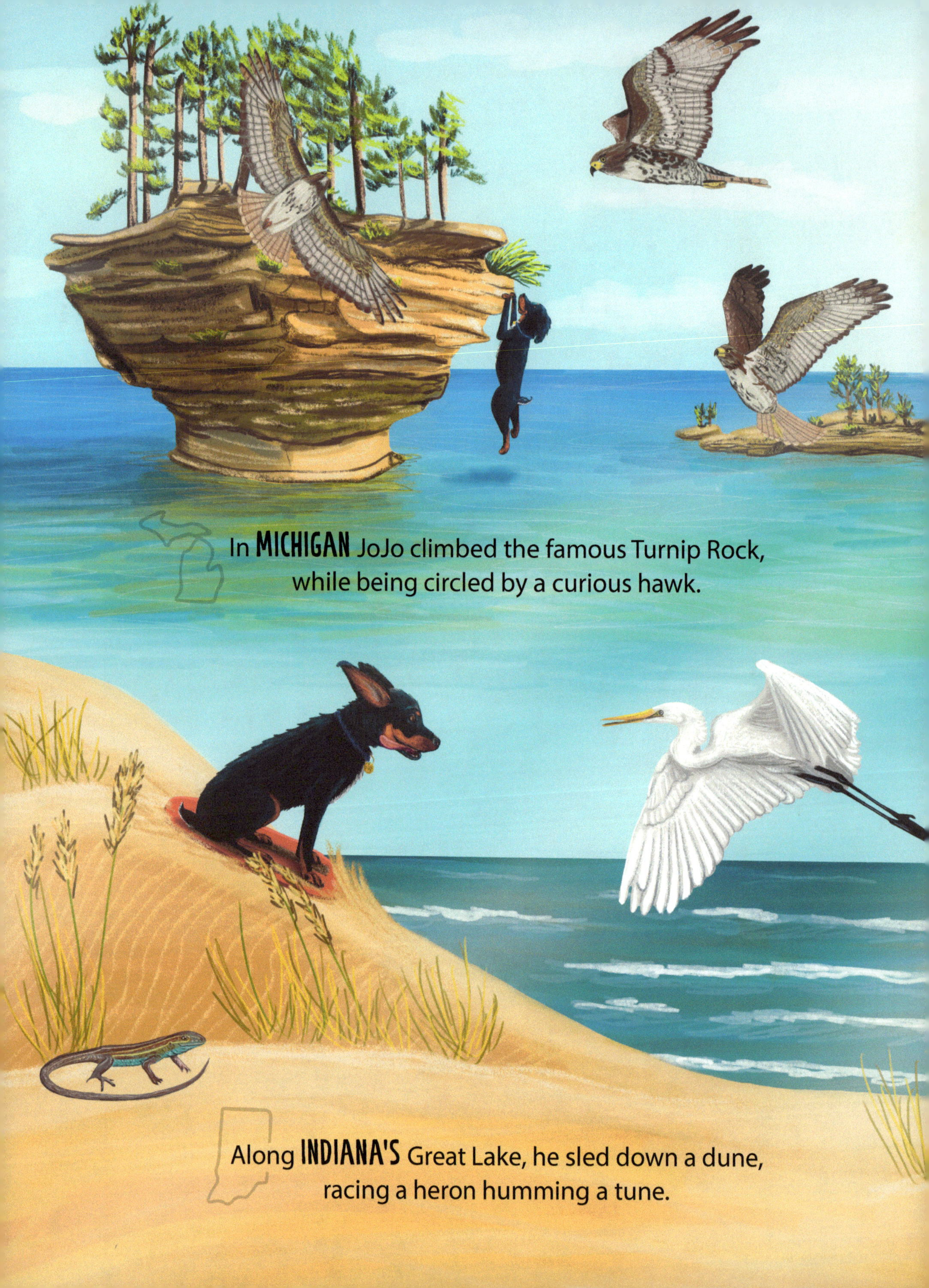

In **MICHIGAN** JoJo climbed the famous Turnip Rock,
while being circled by a curious hawk.

Along **INDIANA'S** Great Lake, he sled down a dune,
racing a heron humming a tune.

In **OHIO** JoJo snowshoed with a fox,
whose feet looked covered in black socks.

Up **WEST VIRGINIA'S** New River Gorge he climbed so high
that an eagle flew up to meet him in the sky.

In WASHINGTON DC JoJo paddled in a large swan,
to see the cherry blossoms along the Monument's lawn.

On MARYLAND'S bay he peered over the side of a dock
finding two blue crabs with their claws locked.

In **DELAWARE** JoJo was floating in the waves,
when he was splashed by a dolphin named Dave.

To **NEW JERSEY** he hiked along Paterson Great Falls,
while Monarch butterflies surrounded him, big and small.

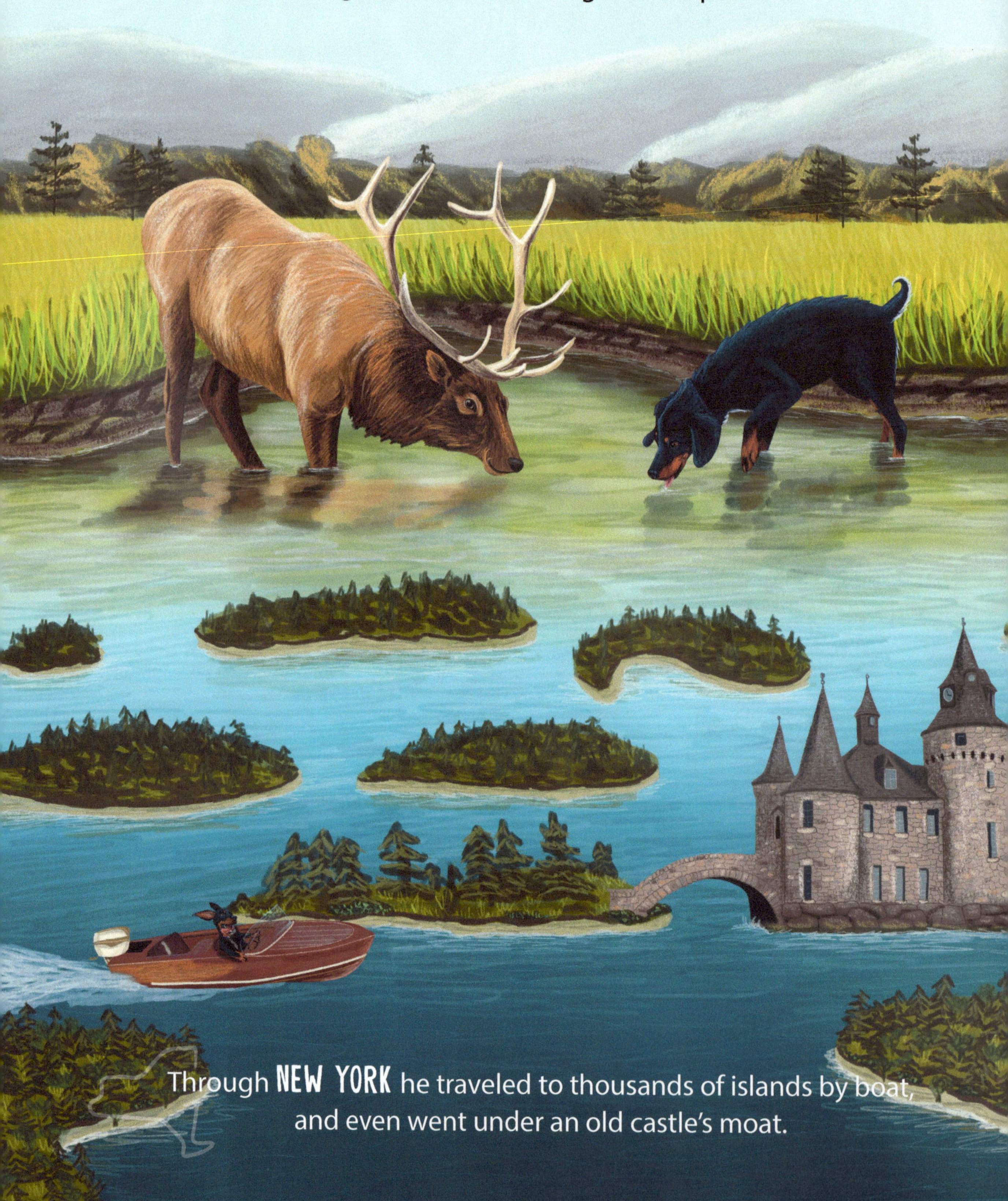

In PENNSYLVANIA JoJo drank from the watered grounds
alongside an elk that weighed 700 pounds!

Through NEW YORK he traveled to thousands of islands by boat,
and even went under an old castle's moat.

In CONNECTICUT JoJo hauled lots of logs
to help build a dam with a beaver named Bog.
Under RHODE ISLAND he dove where the mako sharks feed,
diving and jolting with great speed.

In **MASSACHUSETTS** JoJo posed with a silly hat,
in front of a lighthouse with Tia the Pirate Cat.

Down **VERMONT'S** snowy slopes he caught some air,
then quickly raced back to the ski lift chair.

In NEW HAMPSHIRE JoJo looked out the window of a train,
at the bright fall colors that painted the terrain.
Up north to MAINE JoJo relaxed on Acadia's rocks,
when a seal popped up and gave him a shock!

After his travels across the map,
JOJO THE ADVENTURE PUP curled up for a really big nap.

As he slept, he smiled at all he'd seen.
His BIG ADVENTURE like a wonderful dream.

JOJO THE ADVENTURE PUP
in real life!

1. ALAKSA
Iditarod Historic Trail

2. CANADA
British Columbia's Inside Passge

3. WASHINGTON
Nooksack River

4. OREGON
Cannon Beach

5. CALIFORNIA
Redwood National Park

6. HAWAII
North Shore, Oahu

7. ARIZONA
Painted Desert

8. NEVADA
Lake Mead

9. UTAH
Neon Canyon

10. IDAHO
Rocky Canyon Springs

11. MONTANA
Flathead Reservation

12. WYOMING
Yellowstone National Park

13. COLORADO
Mount Elbert

14. NEW MEXICO
Albuquerque

15. TEXAS
Paulo Duro Canyon

16. OKLAHOMA
Wichita Mountains National Wildlife Refuge

17. KANSAS
Kansas City

18. NEBRASKA
Toadstool Geologic Park

19. SOUTH DAKOTA
Badlands National Park

20. NORTH DAKOTA
Maah Daah Hey Trail

21. MINNESOTA
Lake Superior

22. IOWA
Maquoketa Caves

23. MISSOURI
Ozark Trail

24. ARKANSAS
Bear Cave Trail

25. LOUISIANA
The Atchafalaya Basin

26. MISSISSIPPI
Natchez Trace Parkway

OSS-COUNTRY ROUTE

27. ALABAMA
Dauphin Island
28. FLORIDA
Blue Spring State Park
29. GEORGIA
Appalachian Trail
30. SOUTH CAROLINA
Congree National Park
31. NORTH CAROLINA
Corolla
32. TENNESSEE
Great Smoky Mountains
33. VIRGINIA
Birch Knob Tower
34. KENTUCKY
Mammoth Cave
35. ILLINOIS
Jackson Falls
36. WISCONSIN
Pope Farm Conservancy
37. MICHIGAN
Turnip Rock
38. INDIANA
Indiana Dunes National Park
39. OHIO
Cleveland Metroparks
40. WEST VIRGINIA
New River Gorge
41. WASHINGTON D.C.
Tidal Basin
42. MARYLAND
Chesapeake Bay
43. DELAWARE
Delaware Bay
44. NEW JERSEY
Paterson Great Falls
45. PENNSYLVANIA
Elk County
46. NEW YORK
Thousand Islands
47. CONNECTICUT
Connecticut River Valley
48. RHODE ISLAND
Atlantic Ocean
49. MASSACHUSETTS
Annisquam Lighthouse
50. VERMONT
Killington
51. NEW HAMPSHIRE
Conway Scenic Railroad
52. MAINE
Acadia National Park